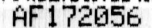

MIRRAN THOUGHT

MIRRAN THOUGHT
Spitzwiesenstr. 50
90765 Fürth
Germany

www.dwmirran.de
www.empty.de
empty@empty.de

READ FIFTEEN
(MT-599)

Printed and published by
BoD - Books on Demand,
D-22848 Norderstedt
www.bod.de
info@bod.de
ISBN 978-3-7412-6424-5
First printing 2016

MIRRAN THOUGHT is the publishing arm of Mirran Threat, a company devoted to releasing the music and writings of the various members of Doc Wör Mirran. Mirran Thought and Mirran Threat are both divisions of MT Undertainment.

Junior Blues

Joseph B. Raimond III

Written in Fürth, Germany in 2016, except "Junior Blues" written in Fürth, Germany, Gardone Riviera, Italy and San Diego, California. "Atlanta Ground" was written in Atlanta, Georgia. "Not From You" was written in Paris. "Turtle Blurter" was written in Barcelona.

As always, in loving memory of Frank Abendroth and Tom Murphy.

For Conny, my perfect angel

Dedicated to Joseph Raimond Jr.

Cover art by Joseph B. Raimond "Claustrophobia" watercolor and ink on paper, 2016 Fürth

This is DWM release Nr. 143

Junior Blues

Please forgive me,
This probably vain attempt
For a few brief moments of immortality
As you lie on your deathbed, I think
Of you

Happy not to have to see
How age and regret, ravaged your life
Up to these last minutes, as you drift away
Happy for you, that you are not in pain
Happy for you, that you got that right
If not much else

You know how I am, better than anyone
Not to want to see the so-called progress
Of modern, medical technology
I am your son, after all

It doesn't matter what road one takes
The destination is always the same
Some of us just arrive earlier than others

Some of us are given an easy road
Some of us take the long, hard road
You chose the road called sadness

Distance and other people's routine
Ruin the best intentions
Not that your intentions were ever all that good

And the mighty dollar,
America's one true god
The one you really pledged your allegiance to
Well, where is it now, when you need me?

Who am I kidding?
You never needed me

If creative is creation, does that make me a god?
For only when I create do I feel immortal,
But still, like any of this could ever mean anything
To anyone

It didn't mean that much to you
And you certainly
Would never have read this book

Is this divine enough for you?
Weren't we always really speaking
The very same language?

But at least I'm not addicted to my own sorrow
But at least I know the meaning of passion
Like a word from another planet
I don't think you ever felt what the word means

Can a person be passionate about regret?
If so, you were the champion
But could not color nor form
A well placed word
Or an inspiring melody
Not plant a small seed of passion?
Not in your soul, ever

Or were your thoughts
So full of regret and remorse
So grey with indifference
That no art could ever shine
And cast rays of hope and love
Onto your saddened soul?

Happiness is at most a very temporary distraction
A bad joke, like quicksilver always darting away
From our vain and futile attempts at grasping
Something that might give us just a moment
Of meaning

We, the living are the ultimate losers
The dead the lucky
And the never born the lottery winners
Who never have to look in a mirror and wonder
Who the fuck is that old man looking at me?

Damn you,
Damn you, damn you,
For exiting so quickly, with so much

Left unsaid

Your death makes no difference
You never called me in thirty years
You aint gonna call me now
So what is the difference?

And today, your conservative
Unwanted ghost
Follows me, annoys me, taunts me
Wherever I go

Even though I doubt you ever saw these shores
These waters lapping onto a culture
Of a thousand years
Some of it even in your rotting blood

No, you never saw these waters
Through caring eyes
Drank of the wind and the art
Of pretty girls walking by
Tasted of the culture
You so like to claim, you Italian stallion you
Was in your blood
As you often so boasted
No, you wouldn't have cared even then

In your hatred of a liberal Europe
You would only laugh
At the coming Muslim invasion, calamity

You so wrongly predicted
Through your eyes of patriotic intolerance

Why did you even bother trying
To understand spirituality?
You would have made a much better
Atheist

With all your scorn and hate

Never, ever
Willing to lift a finger
Give a dollar
Offer a helping hand
Open your heart
To anyone

You gave your religion a bad name
And I am sure
Take it from an atheist, liberal
Pussy whipped European
(Your words, not mine)
That if there is a heaven
Then you,
More than anyone
Aint there!

So, who pressed the fast forward button?
One minute, I'm playing outside
The next, I'm watching you going into the ground

I look in the mirror and think
Who the fuck you lookin' at
You ugly old man?!?
You look so much like your father

In the end, you only polluted our skies
Not a lot unlike how you polluted our minds
And now you are neither here, nor there

For your heaven doesn't exist
Which you proved better than anyone
Nor the hell which you so feared and
In the end deserved

You are nowhere
Except here in our minds,
Wasting more of our thoughts than you ever deserved.

In the end, what did you ever give me?
A life that I never asked for?
Big fucking deal

None of the money you didn't have

Nor your shack, four walls
Fit for the gloom that lived there
Nor your nice, American made
Japanese car
(remember to buy American!)

No, all I ever wanted from you were
Three simple words

But that was too much to ask
And you gave me nothing

In all that time, so many years
All I ever wanted
Was for you to show me
That I meant something to you

For over thirty years
I never had the guts
To tell you
That I love you
Now I'm glad I didn't

Back Seat

Driving home from somewhere
It got late
Mom and dad in the front seats
Talking quietly

With the vicious and cold
Rain pelting the roof of the car
The windshield wipers working furiously
Letting dad see the dark road ahead

Little sister and I
In the back seat
Getting sleepy,
Falling asleep slowly
Our daddy,
The best driver in the world
Will protect us
And keep us warm

We sleep finally
Knowing that nothing can hurt us

So many, many years ago
I long for those few moments
When time was not my mortal enemy
And I still thought my daddy loved me

Joseph & Mary

So ironic
As you sped through the night
With infidelity in your heart
Anger in your mind
You wanted to take your life

Cheating, in your heart, not only
On your love
But also your son
Your daughter
All of whom, wanted you
Needed you

And when Mary rejected you
On that lonely night so long ago
We were not enough for you
Were never enough for you
As you wanted to end it all
And take this Mary, and her little child
With you into death

But, like always,
You didn't have the guts
Were too spineless

Broken hearted, you went home
To wife and kids, waiting
Admitted to them all
How you were such a loser
You couldn't even get infidelity right
Too scared to actually kill yourself
(a suicide chump, as Zappa would say)

A lifetime later
Saved and reborn
As you stood preaching your twisted
Interpretations of the bible
To a broken family, all destined for hell

I hope the irony
Of Joseph and Mary
Was not lost on you

Fairborn, Ohio

The monsters were never under the bed
But in a little boy's mind
As he lay in bed and cried
As he lay in bed and tried
To escape from the clutches
Of an infinite gloom
That was slowly
Swallowing him, whole

When he needed protection
And understanding
The most
He was left alone with his fears
Left alone to fight a war
A ten year old could never understand
Or win

And then
When the ringing in his ears
Got so loud
Even drowning out his heartbeat
"Be quiet, I can hear you breathing"
Was the most understanding
He ever got
From a man born without a heart

Day after day,
He pretended to play,
Like a ten year old should

Day after day
He ran from the gloom
No ten year old should ever know
But he always would

Not a daddy in sight

Belts

Always on the move
Driving across states
Always ending one life
Driving, then beginning the next

I had no home, I have no home
I have no feeling of a home

I only felt alone
Always the new kid in class
"You look funny!"
"Why do you have red hair?"
"Are you part albino?"

And after a third move
Within a single school year
I was the one that was dumb
Too stupid to understand, you said
Always testing your non-existent patience
As you helped me with my homework

Bringing home a bad grade,
You sensed my fear
And as I stammered
That I lost my paper
So, you removed your belt

Obviously, this is how a real man
Raises his children
With the iron first of authority

You made me pull down my pants
And lean over the bed
And then you beat your ten year old son

Did you learn this from one of your other
Macho, fellow officers?
Or did it just feel good
To abuse your child for once?

And after sobbing in pain
Only then did I show you my paper
Which I did pass, by the way
And you hugged me and made
Some lame excuse why
You had to hurt me
And I was even more confused
Than before

And two weeks later
Your daughter, only eight
Came home an hour or so later than she had
Promised
And off came the belt
And loud came the sobbing
As you again pretended to be a good
Parent

And I sat in my room next door
Quiet, not making a sound
Glad it wasn't me this time

And to this day
Your daughter and I
Even in your death
Have never, not once
Ever mentioned

Belts

Red Taillights

A little boy
Making little boy noises in the back seat
Of the family car
Getting on your nerves

So you stopped the car
Dragged him out of the car
Drove away
And left him standing
On the side of the road

Oh sure,
You came back
And muttered something
About teaching him a lesson
And yes, that little boy
Did learn something important that day:
He learned that his daddy was a mean
Son of a bitch

Like Mother, Like Son

I was a child
And your mother was dying
I can't remember her name
I won't remember her name
That would be giving her too much credit
History owes it to us
To let her be forgotten to eternity

A grandma not worthy of the word

And when she finally died,
I went out to play with my friends
Because she meant nothing to me

And in her death all those years ago
(Like your death not long ago)
Old memories resurfaced
And you hated her even a little bit more
For all that she never said,
Never did for you

Only
For what she did
To you

And in pain,
You promised yourself and your children
You would not hurt us
Like your mother hurt you
You would show love to your children
Equally

You would die without regrets

Yeah, right

Broken Heartless

Steered towards hate by
Patriotic idiots
You were always easy to steer
Too weak to follow
Your own path

Christian whores abusing their bible
To justify their hatred of mankind
Their sexist, racist and nationalistic
Dogma, you swallowed
Such an easy target, you
Wrapped it up nice and pretty
In a Christian context
And then wondered why no one
Wanted to talk to you anymore

These bastard Christian leeches
Each writing their New York Times bestsellers
You swallowed their ugly patriotic dreck
Like the emotionally starved
Christian you thought you should be

Not lifting a finger for anyone
You judged every man through your
Filter of false Christian hate

Deadbeats, illegals, Moslems
Gays, artists and musicians
And god forbid, atheists
And all the other false Christians

Your own children

All going to hell, all going to hell
Only you will go to heaven

Alone in heaven
Without your children
(your words)
Without your friends
(you never had any friends)
Maybe, just maybe
What you called heaven
In reality is called hell?

Two Strikes, You're Out!

After your virgin whoring
You released your souls to this world
Never once asking them
If they wanted to be born

You barely swung
Before your first strike
What a failure, what a total loser
(at least I know how to spell it!)

You gave up and moved on
Tried a little bit harder
On the second pitch
But not much
Before your second strike
Bigger loser

Then when the bitterness set in
Amid boos and sneers
You gave up,
Simply walked away from the game
The biggest loser

Sitting alone and sulking
Giving everyone else
Your unwanted, useless rules and opinions
On how to play the game

US Airforce. Vietnam.

Lame

A few months of boozing 'n broadin'
Not a war trauma in sight
And this is what eternity
Is supposed to remember you for???

How about how you saved
A little soul's life
Who today is out there
Living her life to the fullest
Making her mark on the world
Only because of you

Or how about
Helping those that can't help themselves
Showing them how to live in this world
How to be happy, how to care
Only because of you

Oh, I have to admit, it's only fair
That you did
Some good for this world
Maybe even a lot

You left your mark
In a way that matters most
In a way that most of us
With our petty, abstract attempts
At immortality
Will never, ever achieve

Too bad eternity
Was too fucking stupid to notice

Not From You

I learned to love
The written word
      But not from you

I learned to find passion
In the melody
Of a beautiful song
      But not from you

I learned to feel
The exhilaration
Of an aggressive punk anthem
      But not from you

I was taught
To be deeply inspired
By the color and form
Of a beautiful painting
      But not by you

I was taught
How to love a beautiful woman
      But not by you

I learned the value
Of lifetime friendships

And how to love my fellow man
    But not from you

I learned to fight
For equality
Of race, religion
Or sexual orientation
    But never from you

I learned how
To love my children
Unequivocally
And without question
    But never from you

I am learning how
To respect this earth
To help save it
For future generations
    But not from you

I am still learning
How to say no
And not let everyone
Fuck me over
    But not from you

I have learned
To rise above ignorance
To nurture a hunger

For knowledge
>But not from you

I am still learning
How to become immortal
Through my art
>But not from you

I learned how to love and respect
And care for animals
Who give us so much
And ask for so little in return
>But not from you

I learned how to
Travel through this world
With open eyes
And to be humbled by foreign cultures
>But not from you

I have learned
That to be an American
I don't have to be a
Gun toting, ignorant redneck
>But not from you

I learned how to be a typical teenager
Smoke my first cigarette
Get drunk the first time
>But not from you

I learned how to taste and admire
An old whisky
And to care for a hangover the next day
    But not from you

I learned how to fall in love
And kiss my first girlfriend
    But not from you

I learned how to fight
Uncontrolled patriotism
And brainless nationalism
    But not from you

I learned how to distrust
All government
And to always question authority
    But not from you

I have learned
How to dream
And even fulfill a few of them
    But not from you

I am still learning
Not to be bitter and jaded
And how not to hate myself
    But not from you

I have learned
To loathe and despise death
    But not from you

I am still learning
That spirituality can take so many forms
That one must never stop looking for answers
    But never from you

I have learned
Perhaps the hard way
To be an individual
And to accept
That I am unique
And that that is okay
    But not from you

I have learned
All by myself
How to avoid the pull of gloom
To wait out those dark days
And sometimes
Even feel a bit of happiness
    But not from you

I have learned
How to be the person
That you should be proud of
    But not from you

I Imagined

I imagined a world without countries
Your rage at my un-American indifference
To your crayon borders
Made though of steel and concrete
Cemented with hate and
Stupid national pride
Which would make any East German proud
Oh, how Europe spoiled the patriot in me!

I imagined a world without religion
Too bad as you said, you will never
Meet one of your children in heaven

Yeah, right
As if you were going to heaven
But at least
I have nothing to kill or die for

I imagined a world without hunger
Where the billions for your bombs and bombers
Tanks and troops
Would feed the hunger of your exploitation
So many times over
But no, fuck them, they are all deadbeats

Or Muslims,
Who deserve hell anyway

You never noticed, but I was a dreamer
Because you didn't give a shit about my dreams

I imagined no possessions
And yes, I could
And in my heart, every man is my brother
Be he a Muslim, a Christian, an atheist
Be he gay or straight, or somewhere in between
Every man is my brother

Yes, I imagined all the world
Living life in peace
If you had to hate me for that
So be it

Poor Glasses

What poor
Spectacles
Two lenses, typical apparel
For those of us advancing in age
And wisdom
Our eyes can't keep up
With the vision of our fate

These poor spectacles, once hugging
Your bitter and hateful brain
Your gloom and doom
A brain not capable of
Seeing the bigger picture

What poor
Spectacles
Forced to endure
The dreck of Ann Coulter
And the stupid ignorance of Rush Limbaugh
For years
As these words of uncultured hatred
Were brought into focus
For a gloomy and bitter mind

Trying to make it up to them
I offer the poor glasses:
The youthful exhilaration of the beat poets

The drunken street wisdom of Bukowski
The poetic form and mystic color
Of a timeless Paul Klee

These poor spectacles
Are now an ocean away
On this eroding, warming earth
(an invention of the EU you would say,
to control the American economy)

Even more, a universe away
In this culture of art
Humanism and yes, that dreaded
Liberalism

The poor glasses, as if they could
Sigh in relief
Finally, to offer something of value
To one not so jaded
In hate and resentment

These poor glasses
Today happily hug my brain
Instead of yours

Pine Valley

      After your hasty exit from this world
Tying up loose ends
Of emotion in our hearts
We came to your home

      Never our home, we had moved on
Long before
And could see it through
Uncluttered and rational eyes

      And all we found
Were a few thin walls
A container for dusty clutter,
Emotional baggage
And a lifetime's worth of regret
and gloom

      What should have been a castle, was
A shack made of particle board and wood, plastic
And dust

      Home sweet home!

      God bless this mess!

      A shack, besides yourself,
Home only to loneliness and gloom
Your only true children
Dark regret was the housemaid
Bitterness the man in the house

      And now that you are gone forever
Greed and indifference
Can be the new tenants

My
Valley Of The Lost

The usual: a few socks that don't match
My spare house key
Other objects I've been looking for
And wondering about

And you

Like all the other objects of my world
In the present
I look at them, feel them, sometimes
Watch them

Even love some of them

This present
It is everything
We, the living,
Will ever have
There is nothing else
And no amount of searching
Wishful thinking,
Looking for ghosts
Will ever change that

Those that have entered my
Valley of the lost
Are simply gone
In the past, over

What is lost is lost
The dead will always be dead
And that is the most painful
Horror of our lives

I feel no ghosts
Receive no messages
Or derive meaning
From the valley

We the living
Have been gifted
With the ability to think and learn
To love
And question

We the living
Have been cursed
With the ability
To fear our coming
Death

That which is gone
Is gone forever
And no amount of wishful thinking
Or the reading of a holy book
Or the convincing speech
Of a skilled shaman
Will ever change that

Butcher

I learnt my trade well
And after a lifetime of cutting
Hacking and chopping
Letting the blood out
I am getting tired

Splattering my face
With the blood of your questionable morals
The gore of your sadness
And the guts of your gloom
I watch the lights go out
The will to live going last
Finally, lifeless lumps of meat
Indistinguishable from each other
They lie helpless and dead

The blood has spilled
My blade is dull
I have nothing left to say to you
I am no longer so angry
At all your faults and your stupid words

It is time to clock out
And move on

(When I) Dream Of You

When I dream of you
You are kind, loving
You are my daddy again

When I dream of you
You protect me from
That black gloom
That never tires
Of trying to swallow my soul

When I dream of you
You are free of the demons
That so tormented you
Throughout your life
They are banished, nowhere
To be found

When I dream of you
You are happy for once
You laugh, and make me laugh
And I can love you

I Hope

Now that my emotional dust
Has settled a bit
And time has begun
Healing my wounds
I hope
You are not angry at the resentment
That so often
Creeps from my words

As the opposite of love
Is not hate, but indifference
I hope
You see that my often bitter words
Only show that I always cared

Even though, I never understood you
You were a puzzle
I could never solve

And when we clashed
It was always only for
The roads we chose to take
I hope
You see that we were both
Only looking for answers
As our questions were really the same

And although you never said
Those few words that
I always so craved to hear
I hope
That you were proud of me

And as you laid in that bed
So far away, in your last hours
I hope
You knew that my thoughts
Were always with you

And while you were always angered
At my questioning
Of your spirituality
I hope
That you have found
What you were for so long
Looking for
And if there is a heaven
I hope
You are there, and
Have finally found
The peace and happiness
Your bitter spirit
So craved in your life

I hope
That somehow, somewhere
I will see you again

Tortoise Whisperer

We sit as royalty in our little castles
Defining and refining our morals
To custom fit our wishes and wants
Our bank accounts and dreams

Surrounded by a little army of paid yes-men
We fool ourselves, convince ourselves
To see reality as we want to see it
To justify our actions

And when we hurt someone we should love
Well, he was always a fucker anyway
And she was always greedy anyway
Our deception has come full circle
We talk ourselves into righteousness

And the resulting loneliness
We talk ourselves into thinking
It is what we wanted anyway

That no one calls us anymore
No one writes us letters anymore
No one wants to see us anymore
No one wants to comfort us anymore
Well, "whatever, dude"

Yes, god damn, it is what we always wanted
They are no longer good enough for us
Who cares that they will always have each other
It is what we wanted anyway

Stuff!

And so we wallow in our dollars
But there are not enough of them
To keep us warm

And with eyes wide open, we soberly see
That there is no us, just a me

And you have to ask yourself
Just what have I done?
But your damage is done,
Your bridges long burned
So get used to your own voice
It might be the last
That will ever listen

Down to the level of vulgar vocabulary
Twits instead of tweets
Short little jabs at getting in a clever
Last word
That no one will ever give a fuck about
Except you, the queen of fuckers

Don't bother looking for a reasonable day
Either
When your sense of reason
Has long abandoned your conscience
And greed is the dictator
That governs your actions

Why shouldn't it be so?
After all, you had the world's best teacher
In indifference, greed and phony morals
Like father, like daughter as they say
And you graduated with honors!

You are the perfect daughter
To a man you barely knew

Turtle Blurter

Twit twitted
White trash vocabulary
And a kindergarten intellect
Even your father
Would have been ashamed
At what is becoming of you

A poetic whisper
Can never come from a blurt
No matter how hard she tries
So the spoiled angry
Turtle blurter
Throws a fucker here
Throws a fucker there
And then sticks her
Head in the sand

A blurted dude
Augmented by a cold keg
And a lighted joint
Isn't the road to trust
But with her head
Buried so deep in the sand
That is something she will never know

So stop your ugly blurting
And stop throwing
Your ugly, white trash fuckers around
For once, grow up
And at least try
For a poetic whisper

Twisting At The Family Ball

Let's twist again,
Like we did last summer
Let's twist again, like we did last spring
Let's twist it again, till we bend it right
Let's twist it again, till I've convinced myself
        I'm right

    'Cause were twisting
    At the family ball
    I'll stab your back
    If you stab mine
    'Cause were twisting
    At the family ball

Let's cry again
Like we did last autumn
Let's cry again, like we did last winter
Let's cry again, like we're doing
Day for day
Let's cry again, because I know
        I never want to see you again

        'Cause were twisting
        At the family ball
        I'll stab your back
        If you stab mine
        'Cause were twisting
        At the family ball

(awesome Iron Maiden-like Guitar solo!)

Let's die again,
Like we did last summer
Let's die again, like we did last spring
Let's die again, like we're doing over and over
Let's die again, because we can never go back
        To our fairy-tale,
        Of what we never were

Atlanta Ground

Nicely stoned against
That fear of falling
Bouncing down to death, to the earth
As gravity rushes up to meet us,
One way or another

The nightmares continue to roll
Just as the plane, eagles in the sky rolls
And my eyes roll
As I struggle for calm

Plane train, B for Bravo
C for Charlie, D is for David
E for Echo, echo, echo…….
Y'all!

I aint no southerner
But with fear as my guide
Atlanta ground
Even if just a glimpse
Is a fine sight indeed

All the purty colored gurls
Heads of braids and rastas
All good lookin', good cookin'
Good…. Well you know what I mean!

And I sit in drugged contentment
Admiring the midnight tush
Savoring every fleeting minute
Till the scheduled terror
Might bring me home

As the monster birds
Zoom around in confusion
I fail miserably
At wishing them out of the sky

And the busy workers
Working on my grand bird
Have the power of life or death
As I watch their bored faces
Another day
Another minimum wage
Saving for a car, maybe
As I pray for my stoned life

(A worthy) Epitaph

Joseph Raimond Jr.

October 3rd, 1939 – December 29th, 2015

United States Airforce

Father, grandfather
A patriot, a world traveler
He gave life
He saved life
And in his own unique way,
He made his children proud